KAT DOGGERS: SUPERSPY

AUSTIN STACK

A. M. Stack Publishing

CONTENTS

CHAPTER ONE

As Chief Mission Specialist Fisk padded along the hallway of the Feline Undercover Regiment's headquarters, something terrible happened. The lights flickered and went out, and across the base computer screens went dark. Flashing red lights replaced the building's bright glow. Fisk's whiskers tingled, his fur raised, and he tensed.

Moving faster, he continued through the hallways and arrived at the door to the Operations Room —called Ops, for short. Placing his paw on the scanner, he entered. Everywhere in the room, cats spun in circles, chasing the red warning lights on the floor and walls. Fisk shook his head. No matter how well-trained they were, the cats couldn't ignore a bright light or a fluffy feather to play with.

"What's happening?" he asked the room full of operatives, but no one responded.

Groaning, Fisk moved to his computer, where he tried to figure out the problem. After a few minutes, he got the screen to turn on, but he only saw one image: a laughing cartoon dog.

Fisk's eyes narrowed and he turned to one of the other agents in the room. "Jim, call in the agents."

"Which ones?" Jim asked, looking up reluctantly from the light he had been chasing.

"All of them," Fisk said. "This means trouble."

Kat Doggers was an ordinary house cat. Well, almost. She was also the newest recruit in the Feline Undercover Regiment, also known as F.U.R, and she was about to get her first assignment.

On that particular day, Kat lay in the house, bored. To pass the time, she sat on the edge of the living room couch and talked to Sam, the dog. He had appeared one day when the humans came home from a long day out. They had gushed to Kat that he had joined their "family".

First, Kat had wanted to declare, *There is no us. I am a one-woman show. And second,* he *is* not *joining us.*

They didn't seem to understand, and Sam never left, so Kat tried her best to ignore the silly mutt. She avoided his company and took every chance to get the pooch in trouble.

Sam had no idea that his fellow pet had joined a crime-fighting spy agency, and Kat wanted him to stay that way. Her identity was top-secret.

"So when do you think the humans will get back?" Sam woofed, rolling on the hardwood floor until he banged his head against the wall in his excitement.

Kat rolled her eyes at his antics. "Five o'clock, same as usual. Why are you so eager to see them today?"

More eager than usual, at least, Kat thought.

Sam always loved seeing the humans. Kat preferred to be more dignified. The humans should run to greet *her*, not the other way around.

Rubbing his head with a paw, Sam gave her a look that said, *You have to be kidding me.*

"You know why," he replied.

"Oh yeaaah..." Kat said, suddenly remembering the date, but smiling as if she knew the whole time. "Today's the anniversary."

"Two years ago today, they adopted me," Sam sat up proudly, "And tomorrow morning we'll celebrate with cake for them and dog treats for me. I can't have any of the cake, of course, because they wanted a fruitcake and dogs aren't allowed to eat grapes because they are dangerous."

"Yeah, you have fun." Kat said, her ears flattening onto her head as she tried to ignore him.

She folded her front paws as the front door opened and Sam ran to greet the humans.

They never throw parties for me, Kat thought, watching as Mom and Dad petted the dog and made baby noises at his face. The bunches of balloons they held bobbed up and down, and she wrinkled her nose at them.

In that moment, Kat got mad. She hissed and swiped at the closest balloon with her paw. As her claws came out, she hit the balloon and it popped, making the others jump.

"Kat" Mom scolded. "Bad kitty!"

Kat shrank back. "What? He deserved that."

But as the woman lifted her and carried her to the other room, she saw the sadness on Sam's face and felt guilty. Mom put her down on the floor and wagged a finger at her, and then she turned and left, closing the door behind her and trapping Kat in the study.

Kat hopped onto the big desk in the middle of

the room and curled into a ball on top of the warm computer. For a second, she felt bad about being mean on Sam's special day, but then she shook her head. Ugh.

Suddenly, Kat sat up as her neck started to vibrate. The F.U.R. communicator built into her collar rang with a sound only her sensitive ears could hear. She had a mission!

CHAPTER TWO

Getting out of the house to go on her mission would be much harder now that Kat had to escape her time out. She looked around the study, searching for a way to escape. If she took too long, she wouldn't get to F.U.R. headquarters in time for the briefing!

She spotted a cup full of pencils on the other side of the desk and pounced, grabbing three of the pencils in her mouth. Then, she turned and scampered over to the edge of the desk closest to the study window. Kat leaned forward, shifting to get a good position. Once she locked on her target, she sprang over the gap between the desk and the wall, landing on the windowsill gracefully.

She wedged the pencils into the bottom of the

closed window and tried to push them down. After several tries of bouncing on the wooden sticks, they snapped in half under her weight. With a harrumph, Kat leapt back over to the desk. This time, she grabbed a pawful of pens and brought them over to try again. The pens did not break when she pushed on them, but they did bend and become useless.

Kat groaned and looked back over at the desk. "One more try."

Finally, she took some of the thick colorful markers that the boys used to use. These days, the tips were bone-dry, but they would work fine for what she needed. After replacing the pens with the markers, Kat again pushed down on the ends that stuck out. At last, the window slowly began to move. She pushed harder, pressing her paws down as much as possible, until she'd opened a big enough space for her to squeeze through.

Kat snuck out through the open window and entered the garage through the pet flap.

"I am a genius," Kat chuckled as she pulled her human Brody's skateboard out through the flap into the street and climbed on.

On her last visit to HQ, she had made sure to have one of the techie cats in the Gadget department fit the skateboard with hidden rocket boosters to let her ride to work, rather than getting her paws dirty on the pavement. The rockets had been programmed to activate by way of her paw print, so that Brody would never send his skateboard flying off into the distance with him aboard!

She activated the rockets and sped towards F.U.R. headquarters.

KAT'S HEART POUNDED AS SHE ARRIVED AT THE normal-looking office building that housed F.U.R. headquarters. Her first mission briefing! She walked to the back of the building, where a brown door mouse named Zak greeted her with a tip of his flat blue hat. The cap had the agency's signature logo, a ball of yarn with a pawprint in the middle, sewn into the fabric. He looked delicious, but eating Zak would be against the rules. She gave him a wink instead.

"Good morning, Agent 32. Password?"

"Curiosity," Kat replied, and Zak nodded.

"Enter," he told her, stepping aside and revealing a plain brick wall. A square part of the wall glowed and became see-through, like glass. The high-tech cat flap slid upward into the wall.

Wish I had one of these at my house, she thought as she padded through.

Kat stepped into the agency's main lobby. The tall, rectangular room had colorful walls and the F.U.R. logo on the far wall. Normally, bustling cats filled the space, swapping stories about their latest missions, but today the entire place stood empty. Kat dashed for the front desk, a huge semicircle filling the far end of the room. When she reached the front, one of the ten receptionists told her to head to Ops; the Operations room.

The rest of the base was as empty as the lobby. Kat scampered down the echo-ey halls until she arrived at the large door labeled "Operations". She raised a paw and scratched at the door, but nobody answered. Fidgeting with her tail, Kat scratched the door again. Still nobody came.

"Hey," someone said from behind her. Kat turned to see a calico carrying stacks of documents down the hall. "The briefing is already over. All the agents have left."

"You mean, I missed the mission?" Kat asked. She looked past the other cat to see a group of other young, inexperienced agents heading down the hall and disappearing around the corner.

"I guess so," the other agent shrugged. "Hope you don't get in too much trouble."

"Oh man," Kat cried, pushing past the calico and

chasing after the other rookies. "What do I do now?" If she hadn't popped Sam's balloon, she wouldn't have been running late. This was all her fault.

She turned the corner and found herself in an empty hallway that ended in a fork with two different paths. Kat looked back and forth, trying to figure out which way the team had gone. She saw that the left hallway had a big red sign that read:

LEVEL THREE ZONE
ACCESS RESTRICTED TO AUTHORIZED
AGENTS ONLY

"I haven't worked with you since that operation in Poland," a voice came from one of the rooms further down the left passage.

"Try not to get me caught by an angry mailman this time," came the reply. "You guarded that big meeting between the cats and dogs of the city, right?"

Kat's ears pricked up at the sounds of the voices. She glanced at the restricted sign again—she was only a Level One agent... But she recognized those voices, and so she padded past the sign to the open door, and peeked into the room.

CHAPTER THREE

The room reminded Kat of a human theatre, with three rows of seats before a stage. A screen covered the back wall behind the stage. Two figures sat in the front row. Kat couldn't see their faces, but she would recognize those two agents anywhere. On the right-hand side sat Emily Doggers, Kat's older cousin. Emily had the same tawny fur as Kat, although her paws were white-tipped and she looked much more elegant. Next to her sat a tuxedo-patterned tomcat: Ace Knight, the best spy in the world. Those two had been Kat's idols for years! They had inspired Kat to join F.U.R. in the first place!

Onstage, the absent-minded Mission Control Operator, Mr. Fluffles, started the briefing. The old cat wore large, circular glasses and had fluffy, gray-white fur. He became distracted so often that Kat had no idea how he did his job.

Mr. Fluffles cleared his throat. "Alright, Agent Doggers, Agent Knight, here's what we know. Last week, at a major conference where the city's cats and dogs sat down to negotiate a peace treaty and stop fighting with each other, someone stole and ate the food and wrote gross insults all over the walls of the ballroom while nobody was looking.

"Then, this morning at 0800 hours, an outside force hacked and shut down F.U.R.'s security mainframe, displaying this symbol when they did." An image of a laughing dog appeared on the screen behind Mr. Fluffles. "We don't... Oh hey, Ace." Mr. Fluffles waved a paw at the audience. "I like your hat. Don't you think he has a cool hat?"

Kat had to admit he had a point. The hat looked pretty cool—quite colorful and triangle-shaped.

Emily piped up, trying to get the meeting back on track. "Alright, well, how about we turn the stage over to Agent Fisk. Fisk, what are your thoughts?"

"It's a nice hat, I won't lie, but I couldn't pull it off myself," the grey-furred cat named Fisk told her, stepping forwards. He wore a black tie and a pair of thin, rectangular glasses.

"No, about the *mission*," The agent cried, frustrated.

"Oh! Right, yes," Fisk nodded. "So, we traced the signal of the hack to an old mansion outside of the city, and we'll be sending you in to try and find the person responsible."

"Seems like we already know who is responsible," Agent Knight commented. "We've seen that symbol before."

"The Ha-Ha Hounds..." Emily muttered, folding her paws.

Fisk nodded. "True. This seems to be yet another trick pulled by the infamous gang of criminal dogs known as the Ha-Ha Hounds. We know they don't want cats and dogs to be friends. They want to be able to fight cats whenever they want."

"Why are we the only ones on this mission?" Emily asked. "That gang is dangerous."

"We have nobody to spare. All of the other agents are being sent to round up the Ha-Ha Hounds' minions at their bases in the city," Fisk explained. "If we're right, though, the Hounds' leader is hiding here at this mansion. You two are the best of the best, so we're sending you to capture them."

"They've been making all sorts of trouble for the

past three weeks," Ace declared. "Now they've gone too far and attacked the first major peace meeting between the cats and dogs of the entire city!"

"But you caught their leader already," Kat said aloud. "Bellowin' Bobby has been in jail for ages!"

She froze, realizing her mistake as the four cats in the room spun to stare at her. Sheepishly, she stepped forward through the doorway and smiled.

"Kat?" her cousin exclaimed. "What are you doing here? This area is off limits!"

"Agent Doggers the Younger," Fisk said. "You are supposed to be on a different mission right now."

"Well, you see," Kat stammered, "I came late and I sorta missed the briefing, but look—"

"You what?!" Emily cried.

"Listen!" Kat exclaimed. "You guys are going on a dangerous, elite mission to a spooky mansion in the middle of nowhere."

"Yes..." Fisk nodded.

"You don't have any other agents to spare, and those two need backup."

"Yes," Fisk replied. "But—"

"I have no mission anymore," Kat finished. "So clearly, I am the best choice to help you out."

The other agents exchanged looks.

Emily shrugged. "She has a point."

"Agent?" Fisk asked, turning to her.

"Sir," Emily said, taking a deep breath. "I've seen my cousin in action. She's smart and skilled—maybe she could come along, just to see what the top agents do."

"I've seen her too," the techie cat replied. "She's reckless and impulsive. Every simulation she ever did, somebody got hurt because she rushed in too quickly."

"That's why she needs this!" Emily declared. "If she gets experience with us, she'll learn how careful she has to be on real missions."

"This is an incredibly dangerous mission," Fisk warned her.

"Which is why I want Kat to watch our backs. I'll take responsibility for her," Emily declared. "I'll keep her safe and make sure she does what she's told."

Fisk rubbed at his chin with one paw. "Are you absolutely sure? You'll be the one in trouble if she steps out of line."

Emily shot Kat a glance. "I'm sure."

"Very well." Fisk turned to Kat. "Welcome to the mission, agent."

CHAPTER FOUR

As the team left the briefing room and headed for the hangar bay, where F.U.R. kept their high-tech airplanes and helicopters, Kat couldn't help freaking out a little. She had a place on a super important operation, where she could finally get to work and help save the world. She'd dreamt about this ever since she joined the Spy Academy.

Never in a million years did she expect to be doing her first real mission with Agent Ace Knight, the number one spy in history! She had his poster on her wall inside her covered bed, hidden where the humans couldn't see. Ace Knight had been the youngest F.U.R. agent ever. In just a few years, he had gone on all sorts of crazy missions: he solved the Case of the Empty Pyramid, stopped a crazy mad scientist with a super-laser, and saved the feline rock band World Domination from being catnapped for ransom. He even had his own slick theme song, performed by Parrot Hilton. Kat couldn't help but stare at Agent Knight as he strutted down the hall, head raised high.

When Ace caught Kat watching him, he sniffed at her with a grossed-out expression on his face. "Don't gawk, kid. That's pathetic."

Kat's ears went back against her head and she ducked away from his sunglasses-covered eyes. "Sorry."

"So, Kat," Emily said, walking next to her. "I'm glad you passed training and started working in the field!"

Ace scoffed. "How did a runt like you get into the agency?"

"Well, they recruited me a few months ago after I saved a human from a falling shelf at the vet's office. He had a bunch of dogs on a leash, so I ran in front of them and got them to chase me. They pulled him out of the way and saved him. A F.U.R. agent there for a routine claw clipping saw me and told the big bosses, and next I knew they offered me a job," Kat explained. "Emily vouched for me."

Ace scoffed. "That's all? They pulled *me* out of

the Cat Legion for Armed Warfare. I saw *battle*, little kitty. Have you seen battle?"

Kat backed away as the tuxedo cat leaned his angry face towards hers. "No..." she replied anxiously, "But I did pass training at the top of my class."

"Annoying rookies," he complained as they arrived at the hangar door. "Forget training, furball. Real missions are one million times harder."

He stepped through the door and headed for their jet plane, flicking his tail rudely at Kat as he went. Emily glanced at Kat and sighed before following Agent Knight out the room. Kat sat there for a second, confused, upset, but mostly angry. Her number one hero thought she was a dumb rookie? But... he hadn't even seen her in action.

Kat trudged after them into the big open hangar and headed for their vehicle. The nose of the plane looked like a cat head, and the tailfin looked like a cat's tail. The landing gear looked like paws, and the inside was big and roomy, with enough space for all three cats to fit in seats on either side of the plane (and cats like to have a *lot* of space to themselves). Above the seats, feathers hung on strings from the ceiling, and the agents batted them, preparing for potential combat, as the plane took off.

The agents strapped on G.O.O.S.E. packs (Gadgetry Operated in Order to Sink Easily) as they got close to the drop zone.

"Why does Fisk call these G.O.O.S.E. packs anyway?" Kat wondered. "They're just parachutes."

"Because that name sounds cooler," Fisk said over their radios. Kat jumped in her seat and her tail fluffed in surprise. She didn't know he had been listening. Then, she looked at the other agents, embarrassed.

"Alright, agents," Fisk continued, "In a few minutes, your plane will fly over the mission site. Once you jump out of the plane and parachute to the ground, you will do a standard stealth infiltration and confirm that the Ha-Ha Hounds are indeed inside the house. Only after I give permission will you capture them. Understand?"

"Loud and clear, boss," Ace answered.

"Aye-aye," Emily said.

Kat blinked a couple of times. "Okay."

During the rest of their flight, Ace and Emily turned away from Kat and discussed the peace summit that the dogs had ruined.

"I only left the room for five minutes, and when I came back the food had disappeared and someone had painted nasty stuff all over the walls,"

Ace growled. "They said *Cats Stink*, and *Dogs Rule*."

Emily nodded, looking concerned. "That sounds scary."

He shuddered. "It was horrible."

Kat tuned them out and sat back, running through the facts of the case in her mind. For the past three weeks, meetings between the cats and dogs had been going wrong and the Ha-Ha Hounds's symbol was left behind every time. But none of the F.U.R. agents who were tricked ever saw the culprits, and the Hounds' leader, Bellowin' Bobby, had been captured and put in jail by Ace Knight last year. Something smelled fishy about all this, and it wasn't her lunch. Kat couldn't help but feel like they had missed important evidence.

Her thoughts cut off as the pilot called back to them to get ready. They were about to fly over the mansion. Kat joined the other two agents at the plane's trapdoor, which slid open in the floor and exposed them to the dark, cloudy night air.

Without waiting, Ace Knight jumped out of the plane. "Yahoo!"

Emily rolled her eyes, but followed him quickly, leaving Kat hesitating as the wind whipped her fur. She stared down at the huge drop, trembling. A jump like this in training would be easy peasy, but she'd never done one for real.

Focus, Kat, she told herself. *Show them what you can do.*

She took a deep breath, steadying herself, and then jumped.

Kat spread her paws wide like she learned in training. When she passed through the clouds and could see the big, spooky mansion on the ground below, she pressed a button on her collar to activate her G.O.O.S.E. The parachute popped out and immediately, she felt herself slow down for landing. As she touched the soft grass, Kat thanked her training instructors in her head. Even though cats always land on their feet, that jump would have been way too dangerous without practice.

The other two had already landed and were headed for the house. Kat detached her G.O.O.S.E. and hurried after them.

Ace and Kat waited outside one of the mansion's windows as Emily leapt gracefully into the house to check for guards and traps. After a moment, she poked her head back out.

"Clear," she whispered. "Come on, Ace. Kat, your job is to stay here and guard this window. Make sure nobody escapes while we search the house and grounds."

"Emily," Kat replied, "why are you leaving me stuck with guard duty? I can help, too."

"No," Emily told her. "I'm not taking a rookie straight into what might be the most dangerous operation we've had in months on her first day. Sorry."

"But Em—" Kat began.

"Your cousin put herself on the line for you," Ace interjected. "So quit yowling and stay here, rookie."

Kat fell quiet. "Understood."

Ace jumped into the mansion after Emily and disappeared from sight.

CHAPTER FIVE

Kat curled her tail back and forth as she paced below the window. Her excellent vision let her see the entire wide open lawn that surrounded the manor house, and she looked back and forth without ever letting her eyes stop. While watching for suspicious movements, she tried to sort out the many different emotions in her head.

"I feel guilty," she said quietly, "for hurting Sam and making myself late for my first mission. I feel angry at Emily and Ace, for treating me like a dumb kid who can't do a good job. And..." she stopped moving and looked down at her paws. "And I feel afraid that they might be right. Maybe I *am* just a rookie."

"Wow," said an unexpected voice in her earpiece. "That sounds like a lot."

Kat jumped, her fur standing on end and her tail getting bushy. "Fisk!"

"In the fur," the techie cat replied happily. "Or, uh... in the voice."

"I *have* to learn how to turn off my microphone," Kat muttered.

"Yes," Fisk agreed. "That would be smart."

For the next few minutes, Kat fiddled with her earpiece, but couldn't find out how to shut off her mic. With an annoyed huff, she gave up and decided to walk around the outside of the mansion. She knew Emily told her to stay put, but she had to put her skills to use. Something still felt strange about this mystery.

"Who's Sam?" Fisk asked, breaking the silence.

"Ugh!" Kat put her face in her paws. Then, she sighed. "He's my humans' dog. Today is his special day, and I acted badly because I got jealous. I wanted treats and fruitcake." She looked up and smiled. "Of course, he can't have the cake because it has..." Suddenly, a puzzle piece clicked in Kat's brain. "Fisk, that food from the peace meeting that got eaten..."

"Yes?" the operator replied.

"What fruits were in that food?" Kat asked.

"Hmm," Fisk hummed over the comms. "Strawberries, bananas, apples, grapes—"

"That's it!" Kat exclaimed. "Why would the Ha-Ha Hounds eat from food that had grapes? Dogs get really, really sick from those!"

"Cats do too," Fisk commented. "Honestly, we weren't even sure why those were there, much less who would eat them... We just figured the dogs had no idea how to do an event!"

In that moment, Kat looked back at the window where the other agents had gone into the house. Ace and Emily expected to find a gang of rogue dogs, but someone else was behind this and wanted to frame the Hounds.

"I have to get in there," Kat said. "Ace Knight and Emily Doggers are walking right into a trap."

CHAPTER SIX

K at landed in a dark hallway. She glanced back at the window she'd come through, trying to memorize the location so that she knew how to get back out of the building.

South wall, beside a poster for that old movie, "The Adventures of Mr. Bun", she thought.

She examined the poster, and saw that someone had framed a newspaper clipping about the attack on the peace summit. The photo showed the cats and dogs on either side of the room, shouting at each other about the ruined food and decorations. In the far background of the picture, a small ball of fluff with huge ears stood between the two sides.

"Weird," Kat thought. "Why would a bunny be at that meeting? None of them were invited."

Kat examined the house as she moved on and continued down the hall. The mansion had faded wallpaper, covered in flowers that probably used to look bright and cheerful but in the dark looked creepy instead. The ceiling loomed high above, with chandeliers hanging every few feet. Whenever she passed a window, the light coming in cast twisting shadows on the dark red carpet.

"I don't like this place," she muttered. She passed by the entrance to a narrow staircase and paused to look into it. She guessed those stairs led down into the basement.

Kat crept through the mansion's many rooms, but besides the spooky atmosphere, the building looked normal. She found no sign of the other agents.

Finally, she found herself in a huge central living room with couches along three of the walls. The fourth wall held a huge TV. In the center of the ceiling, a chandelier—bigger than the ones in the hallway—swung back and forth and jingled.

Kat imagined she could feel the whole house creaking, as if the place might come alive at any second. She kneaded the scratchy carpet beneath her paws, her wide eyes scanning the room.

"I don't know what to do, Fisk," she confessed. "This house looks empty."

She heard nothing but static in her earpiece this time.

"Fisk?" she asked again.

No answer. The house must have been blocking her communication signal. She had to figure this out on her own.

"Okay, Kat," she said to herself. "You are Agent Knight, and you're on your way into this mansion expecting to run into a gang of dangerous criminal dogs. Where do you go?"

The spy thought back to her time as a kitten, reading about Ace's adventures. His autobiography talked a lot about the way he solved his cases, and Kat knew that book by heart. In one chapter, the superspy talked about how he never relied on one set of senses. If Ace found the main floor of the house empty and silent like this—if he couldn't see or hear anything out of the ordinary—he would have used his sense of smell! Kat sniffed the air and caught a whiff of a scratchy, tangy scent that she followed with her nose. The smell was faint, as if coming from somewhere far away. Somewhere like...

"The basement!" Kat exclaimed. She turned and began retracing her path back to the stairway from earlier.

Ace and Emily would have gone down there

expecting to catch a pack of dog thugs by surprise, Kat thought as she went. Neither agent realized they had been tricked and that someone else was behind the whole mission—someone who wanted to lure them into a trap. The real villain must have known that if they caused enough trouble, F.U.R. would send their top spies—Ace and Emily—to investigate.

"Who would do that?" Kat muttered to herself as she crept down the carpeted hall. "That's what I don't know. They must be enemies of F.U.R., but I don't remember any of those."

Except, she did! Kat realized that whoever wanted revenge on Ace Knight must have been defeated by him before, and Kat knew *all* of the tuxedo spy's old cases after reading about them in his book. She wrinkled her nose as she thought about the many villains Ace had faced.

Her thoughts paused as she realized that she had found the staircase again. The white-painted wooden steps led down into darkness, but Kat could see a soft orange glow from a light down at the bottom. Carefully, keeping a close eye out for trip wires or trapdoors, she started down the stairs into the basement. She almost coughed as the smell grew stronger, and she realized she smelled smoke from something burning!

"Whoever did this," she said as she hurried down, "had to be smart enough to create this plan to frame the Ha-Ha Hounds. They had to have enough money to buy this mansion as a trap, and they had to have serious computer skills to hack into the agency."

Her tail curled back and forth as she thought about what she'd seen in the mansion so far. She remembered the movie poster she saw on the wall, back where she came into the house. "The Adventures of Mr. Bun", an old black-and-white comedy movie about an unlucky rabbit who faced all sorts of problems as he tried to become successful in the world. She remembered the image from the peace meeting prank, where a small white rabbit lurked in the background of the photo, watching as both sides turned on each other.

A lightbulb switched on inside Kat's brain. At that same moment, her radio crackled, and she heard Fisk's voice come through the static and fuzzy noise.

"Agent Doggers! Can you hear me?" he cried. "We broke through the communications jammer."

"I hear you, Fisk," she replied. "And I know who's behind this. I know who the real villain is."

CHAPTER SEVEN

"What do you remember about that time Ace Knight saved the Statue of Liberty?" Kat asked.

Fisk hummed, which sounded funny over the radio. "He had to stop a gigantic super-laser from melting the whole statue down. This crazy scientist wanted to steal some kind of rare mineral he found in the metal... but I don't remember his name."

Kat reached the bottom of the staircase and peeked out the doorway. If not for her super-sensitive feline night vision, she would have been blind. Even so, the place looked dim and she could barely make out any colors. Her paws felt cold and wet, in the middle of some kind of shallow puddle. The rocky space smelled like burning smoke, but also like... carrots?

"His name," she whispered into her microphone, "is Dr. Bertrand B. Bunnytron."

The basement of the mansion looked like a huge, wet cave—except the stone ground looked smooth instead of rocky like Kat expected. All over the wide open space, she saw strange and unusual devices. Some had long, whirring arms that moved back and forth. Others flashed with brightly-colored lights. Many looked broken, piled in corners and thrown away like trash.

On the other side of the space, a group of screens glowed white. In front of them, a silhouette moved, talking too quietly for Kat to hear. Carefully, she crept out of hiding and started sneaking toward the screens.

"Bertie Bunnytron!" Fisk exclaimed in her ear. "He hated Ace, and he swore revenge once we captured him. He escaped from his cell three weeks ago..."

"Right before this whole case started," Kat mumbled.

At last, Kat got close enough to see the person onstage. She looked up to see a small white rabbit in a big black top hat and a bright red bow tie on some kind of metal desk in front of her. His clothes looked way too big for him, and Kat guessed that he must have stolen them from a human store. He stood about half Kat's height, with beady black eyes. Pens, pencils, markers, and a bunch of blueprints and sketches covered the table he walked on. Behind him, Ace Knight and Emily Doggers hung from the ceiling in chains.

The bunny was in the middle of a dramatic, evil speech to the captured agents, and now that Kat was close to him, she could understand his words.

"You see," the bunny said in a fancy British accent, "I simply had to leave evidence to convince your leaders that the Ha-Ha Hounds committed the crimes. I knew that if I caused enough trouble, F.U.R. would track me down and send their best agents to capture me. Except you two fools expected to find a pack of brainless mutts, and not an evil genius with an inescapable trap!"

"But why ruin the peace talks?" Ace asked. "I don't understand!"

The rabbit suddenly looked angry. "Because everyone cares about helping the cats and the dogs, but they ignore the bunnies. Bunnies like me get chased by BOTH cats and dogs, and nobody ever wants to help us out! So if I ruined the meeting, I could get revenge on you AND the cats AND the dogs all at once! Genius!"

"You'll never get away with this!" Emily cried, wiggling in her chains.

"*Au contraire*, my dear feline," Doctor Bunnytron said. "In one minute, the lava in that tank above you will flow down your chains." He paused, rubbing his furry chin. "Lava moves very slowly. Perhaps I should have used a faster trap. Anyway, once the hot lava reaches you both, I will have two cooked geese!"

"You're crazy, Bunnytron!" Ace shouted. "We're cats, not geese!"

"Yes, I know," the rabbit replied, looking frustrated. "That was a metaphor, I don't *actually* think you are... oh, forget it."

Kat looked up to see that Ace and Emily were hanging from a huge black metal tank on the ceiling of the tall cavern, and their chains were right beneath two small holes in the metal. Through those holes, red-and-orange lava dripped slowly down onto the chains, glowing so much they made Kat's eyes hurt when she looked at them. The burning smell from earlier was way worse, and Kat realized it had to be coming from the lava.

Kat's mind raced. She had to stop this! She had to save the other agents, and according to Dr. Bunnytron, she only had one minute to do it!

"Stay where you are, Kat," Fisk instructed through her radio. "Backup is on the way."

She didn't have time to wait for backup. Kat lifted her chin and decided to solve the problem the only way she knew how: direct confrontation.

"Sorry, Fisk," she whispered, and turned off her radio.

She bunched up her back legs beneath her and sprang out of hiding to land on the desk across from Bunnytron.

"Stay back, you crazy rabbit fiend!" she cried.

Kat heard Ace and Emily gasp when they saw her.

The bunny tilted his head. "Oh my, another agent!"

"Doctor Bunnytron, I presume," Kat declared, trying to copy the evil rabbit's deep voice and British accent, though she felt scared standing in front of an evil genius by herself.

"Kat? What are you *thinking?*" Emily cried.

"You presume correctly," Bunnytron told Kat. He twirled a black cane in one paw. "Who are you?"

"My name is Kat Doggers, and I'm here to stop you," Kat told him as bravely as she could.

Bunnytron chuckled. "Good luck."

CHAPTER EIGHT

Without thinking, Kat pounced and tried to tackle Bunnytron, but the doctor moved fast and dodged. Kat chased him, but each time she got close, he leapt away with his powerful hind legs, launching into the air like a huge, fluffy, irritating bird.

This isn't working, Kat thought. *New plan time.*

"Okay, so wait," Kat said, padding towards the evil rabbit and breathing hard. "I know we're supposed to be fighting, and you're evil and blah, blah, blah, but I have to ask—"

"About my evil plan?" Bunnytron asked with a smirk.

"No, no, I didn't want to ask you that," she said.

"I want to know how you made your voice sound so superior and cool."

"What? Why would you ask him that?" Ace shouted. "He's the *bad guy*! Don't compare notes with him!"

"Why, thank you," Bunnytron puffed out his chest with pride. "I've been working hard on my performance, you know."

"I can tell," Kat replied, inching closer to the two chained agents. "Could you give me some advice on how you practice?"

"Well, the key is practice. You see..." Bunnytron began, but at that moment, Kat sprang into action.

She leapt forward, landing on the top of his hat. Her weight made the hat sink down over the rabbit, trapping him. As he wiggled in the tight fabric, Kat ran over to Ace, grabbing onto his chain to inspect the lock that kept him trapped.

"What are you doing, rookie?" Ace exclaimed. "You don't stand a chance against this villain! You'll mess the whole mission up!"

"Be quiet, Agent Knight," Kat ordered. "You're the one who's captured, so stop yowling and let me save you."

Kat poked a claw into the lock's small circular hole.

She fiddled around for a second, but couldn't manage to get the lock open. Above the agents, glowing red lava started to slide down the chains, making the metal start to melt as it went. The heat grew stronger and stronger, and Kat felt her paws start to sweat.

She turned back around and scanned the area, looking for the key to release Ace. Her eyes went to Dr. Bunnytron, who had managed to pull himself out of the hat and now glared at her.

"Ta-da!" the rabbit declared. "I bet you want *this*."

He reached into his bow tie and pulled out a cylinder-shaped key. Kat's eyes widened.

"Hand over the key, Bunnytron!" she shouted.

The rabbit laughed—Kat felt her fur stand on end at the deep, sinister sound. Bunnytron tossed the key into the air and caught it again. He looked *very* angry.

"You're interfering with my plan, Kat Doggers," the evil genius said. "You didn't want to talk about my superior voice at *all*, did you?"

"Of course not, you maniac!" Kat shouted. "You tied up my cousin and my hero and you're trying to melt them with lava!"

"Go Kat!" Emily cried. "Please hurry!"

Bunnytron wrinkled his nose and folded his fluffy arms. "Huh. There's no need to be so rude."

Kat growled. This rabbit needed to be stopped and she was running out of time! She raced toward him, hoping to snatch the key out of his hand—but then the bunny drew his hand back and threw the metal cylinder through the air.

"No!" Kat shouted. She skidded to a stop and spun around just in time to see the key land in the creeping lava and disappear. Bunnytron had destroyed it.

"Nice going, rookie!" Ace shouted sarcastically. He sounded scared.

The rabbit laughed. "There is no escape for you, agents!"

Kat kicked with her back legs, smacking the rabbit and sending him tumbling off the edge of the table with a wail.

"Aaaah!" Bunnytron hit the ground below with a small thud. "Owwwwww..."

Kat's heart pounded, and the lava continued to fall. It was already halfway to Ace and Emily's heads! She started to panic. Without the key, how could she get the locks open to save them? Maybe she could pry them open, but the keyhole would only fit something long and cylinder-shaped. Where could she find—?

A lightbulb went on inside Kat's brain. She thought back to earlier that day, when she'd been trying to open the study window in her house. She'd used several different items to get the window open! The rookie agent looked down at the desk beneath her—among the papers and invention designs she saw all sorts of different writing tools.

Kat snatched a handful of the tools and looked at them. She saw two colored pencils in yellow and dark blue, three grey pens, and one big, thick orange marker. She remembered her attempts to open the window: how the pencils snapped and the pens bent, but the marker stayed strong.

"What are you doing?!" shouted Ace. "Help us!"

Dropping everything except the orange marker, Kat leapt up to Ace's locked chains and jammed the marker into the keyhole.

"Please, please work," she muttered. Then, she pushed on the end of the marker with every bit of her strength. With a loud *click*, the lock popped open, and Kat dragged Ace out of his chains and onto the desk. "Yes!" she cried.

"Kat!" Emily cried.

The rookie agent stopped celebrating. "Oh yeah," she said. "Sorry!"

She ran to Emily's side and opened her lock as well, pulling her cousin out of the way of the lava just in time.

CHAPTER NINE

The three secret agents lay on the desk for a moment, breathing hard. Then, suddenly, Emily jumped up.

"Bunnytron!" she exclaimed, running to the edge of the desk and looking down at where the rabbit had disappeared.

Kat and Ace joined her, and together the agents saw that the villain was long gone, leaving only his huge top hat behind on the stone floor. They sat back, and Emily scratched at her head.

"Listen, Kat," she said. "We owe you an apology."

Kat looked back and forth at the two agents.

"We treated you like a useless kid," Emily continued, "and not only were we mean, but... we were wrong. You looked at the evidence when we were too overconfident to listen to you, and you saved us from that crazy rabbit's evil plan. I'm sorry."

Ace turned away to inspect the desk, but stopped when Emily elbowed him. "Ow!" The tuxedo cat rubbed his shoulder. "Uh, yeah, you did alright. Not bad for a rookie." Emily elbowed him again. "Ow! I mean, um... thank you, and I'm sorry too, I guess."

"That's OK," Kat said. "I forgive you. Besides, I've still got a lot to learn, and I hope you two will help teach me!"

Ace smirked. "You're gonna have to be the best if you want me as a teacher, rookie."

"I will be," Kat replied. Then, she turned away from the others to look back at the abandoned top hat. "Fisk?" she radioed. "You there?"

"Agent Doggers? Kat? Is that you? Man, I'm glad to hear your voice."

"We're safe, Fisk," Kat replied, relieved and happy. "Mission accomplished."

"What about Dr. Bunnytron?" the techie cat asked.

Kat grimaced. "He got away, but we'll find him. And next time, we'll be ready to stop him for good."

. . .

AFTER SHE AND THE OTHERS ESCAPED Bunnytron's underground lab (Kat discovered he had a pretty fancy elevator installed to get to the mansion), Fisk and several F.U.R. agents had arrived to analyze his lair.

Fisk and Kat watched as agents carted Dr. Bunnytron's inventions away in a F.U.R. carrier, and the mission specialist turned to the rookie agent and said, "You did good work here today, Kat."

"Really?" she asked. "I thought I messed the whole thing up."

"You didn't quite follow orders," Fisk said. "That's true. You got upset with your fellow agents and with your problems at home..."

"I know, I know." Kat looked down at her paws.

"But then you did something only the best agents —and the best people—do," Fisk continued. "You talked about your feelings out loud and worked through them. You saved your team and figured out the whole case on your own. Not bad for a first mission."

"Thanks," Kat replied, looking up again and smiling. "I'm looking forward to the next one."

"You'll be the first person we call," Fisk told her. "Until next time, agent."

. . .

Two hours later, Kat sat on the couch at home, enjoying the anniversary celebrations, and smiling.

As Kat watched, her humans leaned in and blew out the candles on their fruitcake before digging in. Below her, Sam walked up and watched them with her. His tail wagged hard and fast, right next to a colorful, fancy flower pot. She looked down at him, and realized that if she wanted to, she could knock the pot over without anyone seeing. Everyone would believe Sam had pushed the pot over with his tail, and he would get in trouble. She could mess up the party even more than she did before... Kat raised her paw and reached out to touch the pot.

But she didn't want to do that. Her family loved Sam just like they loved Kat, and he loved them back. Instead of pushing the pot down, Kat moved it out of the way of Sam's tail, making sure he wouldn't tip it over onto the floor himself by accident. Acting jealous was wrong, and Kat felt happy with her life... even if she wished she could brag about how she saved lives and defeated an evil genius today. Sometimes, having a secret identity stunk.

"I'm glad you're not in time out anymore," Sam said, looking at her.

"Me too," Kat replied. "Happy anniversary, Sam."

The dog smiled big, and then ran off to eat his special kibbles. Then, a pair of big hands scooped Kat up. She twisted her head to see Brody holding her in a gentle hug. He smiled, his blond hair falling into his eyes.

"I see you hiding here, Kat," he said. He scratched her head, and Kat purred. "We know you're a one-woman show who doesn't need big celebrations like this, but we still love you a lot."

Kat purred louder and thought, *I know*.

As she and Brody watched Sam and the rest of the family enjoy themselves, Kat knew her adventures had only just begun.

THE END

ABOUT THE AUTHOR

Austin Stack is an aspiring young author at only twenty years old. He is a longtime book-lover who decided to thank the world for letting him read by writing stories for others. He loves stories about science fiction, superheroes, and fantasy, and he has a soft spot for cats because he grew up with two! He is pretty sure neither of them are secretly spies...

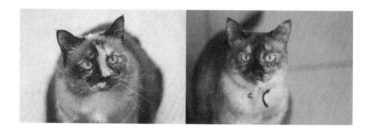

Kat Doggers: Superspy is Austin's first published book, and he can't wait to keep sharing his words.